PARSLEY

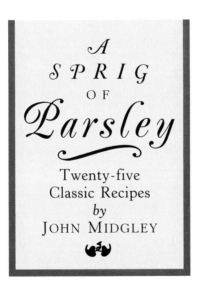

A
S P R I G
O F
Parsley

Twenty-five
Classic Recipes
by
JOHN MIDGLEY

Illustrated *by*
IAN SIDAWAY

A Bulfinch Press Book
Little, Brown and Company

BOSTON · NEW YORK · TORONTO · LONDON

ACKNOWLEDGEMENTS
The author thanks Sue Midgley and Helen Parker for checking the text,
and Ian Sidaway for his excellent illustrations.

FURTHER READING
The Complete Book of Herbs, by Lesley Bremness (Dorling Kindersley)
The Encyclopedia of Herbs, Spices and Flavourings, by Elisabeth Lambert Ortiz
(Dorling Kindersley)
The Herb Book, by Arabella Boxer and Philippa Black (Octopus)
The Herb Garden, by Sarah Garland (Windward)
History of the English Herb Garden, by Kay Sanecki (Ward Lock)
How to Grow and Use Herbs, by Ann Bonar and Daphne MacCarthy
(Ward Lock)
Wisley Handbooks: Culinary Herbs, by Mary Page and William Stearn
(Cassell for the RHS)

First Edition
ISBN 0-8212-2096-9
A CIP catalogue record for this book is available
from the British Library

Conceived and designed by Andrew Barron and John Midgley

Published simultaneously in the United States of America
by Bulfinch Press, an imprint and trademark of
Little, Brown and Company (Inc.),
in Great Britain by Little, Brown and Company (UK) Ltd.
and in Canada by Little, Brown & Company (Canada) Limited

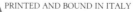

PRINTED AND BOUND IN ITALY

CONTENTS

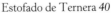

℘ARSLEY

Belonging to the *Umbelliferae* family of plants, and native to southern Europe, parsley was grown by the ancient Greeks who used the herb medicinally and ceremonially, and fed it to their horses. For the Greeks it was also symbolic of death, an association that survived into the Middle Ages. The Romans valued the herb principally as a food and introduced it into Britain. Parsley has remained popular ever since, unlike many other medieval and Renaissance herbs. Undoubtedly parsley is the most widely grown and used of all culinary herbs and has become naturalized in most temperate parts of the world. Its English name is a corruption of the Latin *petroselinum* ('rock-celery') which derives ultimately from Greek.

The three main varieties are *Petroselinum crispum* ('curly' parsley); *Petroselinum crispum Neapolitanum* ('flat-leaf' or 'Italian' parsley); and *Petroselinum crispum tuberosum* ('Hamburg' or 'turnip-rooted' parsley). The first is the most familiar kind which, with its handsome, dark emerald green curled leaves, is reasonably hardy, has a good flavour and is especially attractive as a decorative garnish. Various curly cultivars such as 'Green velvet', 'Champion moss curled', 'Imperial' and 'Suttons curly top' make good ornamental plants. The second variety is the least hardy but is the most aromatic and strongly flavoured. It is the most popular in continental European countries, especially in France, Spain and Italy. However, with the current vogue for Mediterranean ingredients it is becoming increasingly sought-after in Britain and America. The third kind is the

hardiest and will survive the winter. Although the leaves are edible it is grown primarily for its tapering roots which resemble thin parsnips. As its name suggests, it is especially popular in Germany where it is grown as a root vegetable.

Parsley is exceptionally nutritious. All the varieties provide a rich source of vitamins A and C; the minerals calcium, iron and potassium; and chlorophyll, which is thought by many to possess anti-carcinogenic properties.

GROWING PARSLEY

All parsley varieties are self-seeding biennials, producing fewer, smaller and coarser leaves in their second year as the stems lengthen at the onset of flowering. For this reason, they are usually planted annually. Leaf parsley is suitable for planting in physic (medicinal), decorative, all-purpose and kitchen herb gardens. Because it will grow very happily in tubs and pots, troughs and window boxes, it is ideal for small gardens, patios and sunny window sills. Parsley and strawberry pots, peppered with holes that accommodate several individual plants make ideal containers, although ordinary 15 cm/6 inch pots are suitable. Many gardeners like to cultivate curly parsley as an attractive edging plant and to plant it in borders where its decorative foliage contrasts well with coloured blooms. Parsley is also effective in companion planting schemes, particularly with roses.

The tiny crescent-shaped seeds are notoriously slow to germinate; according to one legend the seeds call on the Devil seven times before starting to sprout. Sown outdoors in drills (or directly into containers), the seeds need a warm soil temperature and sowing should be delayed until April or May and can be continued until August (winter crops require the protection of a cloche or cold frame). Many people soak the seeds overnight before sowing. Germination can take over a month and even the Royal Horticultural Society recommends treating the soil with hot water immediately before sowing to hasten the process. A sunny or partly shaded position, in moist, fertile soil that has been well worked with rotted compost or manure is essential. The soil must be regularly watered with a fine rose during germination. Seedlings should be thinned until the remaining plants are about 20 cm/8 inches apart. The plants need regular watering, especially during dry spells. Parsley should be picked as required and although it will grow back readily, you will need several plants to maintain a regular supply. The leaves of second year plants can be prolonged if the flowering stems are removed.

Hamburg parsley is grown from seeds that are sown in March or April, ideally in a shady position in rich, moist soil. The seedlings should be thinned to leave a gap of 30 cm/12 inches between plants. The roots are usually kept in the soil until required; and mature roots have a better flavour than tender ones.

COOKING WITH PARSLEY

With its strong flavour and aroma, flat-leaf parsley is the best variety for adding flavour to food, while curly parsley makes a more decorative garnish. The flavour is most concentrated in the stalks, of which at least a small section should be included when chopping parsley.

Parsley is an essential component of *bouquet garni*, the classical tied bundle of fresh herbs usually added to flavour stews, soups and sauces. Others are thyme, bay and marjoram, and in a more elaborate version, these herbs and a strip of orange peel are tied to a celery stalk. Parsley is also an essential ingredient in *fines herbes*, together with chervil, chives and tarragon. Other classical flavourings are *persillade* (parsley finely chopped with garlic or shallots – see the recipe on page 10) and *gremolata* (chopped parsley, lemon peel, garlic and anchovies); both are added to braised and stewed meat dishes. No good home-made stock (broth) can dispense with the stalks and leaves of fresh parsley. It is also a natural ally of olive oil, seafood, fungi, white sauces, and marinades for meat and poultry.

A relatively fragile herb, parsley loses much of its flavour and scent on drying, so only use fresh leaves and stalks. Whether finely chopped or pounded with aromatics, it is almost always added towards the end of the cooking. The whole leaves make an excellent salad ingredient, and can be chewed to sweeten the breath, being the only effective way to neutralize the odour of garlic with which it is often paired. Hamburg parsley is an excellent root vegetable which tastes like parsley-flavoured celeriac (celery

8

root). It is widely cooked in soups (see the recipe on page 18) but may also be boiled and puréed, or served instead of – or mixed with – carrots and parsnips.

Cut bunches of flat-leaf parsley keep for a few days wrapped in a plastic bag and refrigerated; alternatively, the stale stem bottoms can be snipped off and the bunch crammed into a jug of fresh, cold water. Curly parsley keeps a little longer before fading.

Many of the following recipes are very traditional dishes culled from different cuisines, with a few of my own creations thrown into the pot for good measure.

$\mathscr{P}$ARSLEY BUTTER

Serve little pats of parsley butter on freshly grilled (broiled) steaks which lubricate the meat as they melt. Alternatively, serve with fish or vegetables, or use the butter to baste roasts and barbecues. This recipe makes 8 portions.

110 g/4 oz unsalted butter, at room temperature
½ clove of garlic, peeled and very finely chopped
1 tbs lemon juice
handful of fresh parsley, washed and finely chopped
pinch of salt and freshly milled black pepper

Mash the butter very thoroughly. Mix in the remaining ingredients and mash again. Divide into 8 neat portions and serve. (They may be refrigerated until required.)

$\mathscr{P}$ERSILLADE

A simple mixture of finely chopped fresh parsley and shallots or garlic is added to flavour a wide variety of stews, fish and poultry at the end of their cooking time. In *French Provincial Cooking* (Penguin), Elizabeth David gives recipes for fried aubergines dressed with olive oil and *persillade*, and a Provençale beef *daube* with *persillade* served at the table.

small bunch of parsley, washed and shaken dry
2 yellow shallots, or 3 cloves of garlic, peeled
½ tsp of salt

Chop the ingredients as finely as possible (an Italian *mezzaluna* is a suitable chopping tool). Mix in the salt. Stir the *persillade* into hot, cooked stews and braises, or serve it separately in a little dish.

$\mathscr{P}$ARSLEY MAYONNAISE

Although traditionally whisked by hand, mayonnaise (supposedly first created in the Balearic port of Mahon whence it derives its name) is easily made in a food processor. The eggs must be at room temperature, and it is also important to add the olive oil very gradually. This recipe makes a generous quantity of mayonnaise which will keep in the fridge for a few days if stored in an airtight container.

2 egg yolks
2 tbs lemon juice or 1 tbs wine vinegar
1 tsp salt
small bunch of fresh parsley, washed and finely chopped
225 ml/8 fl oz/1 cup olive oil or a mixture of olive and
sunflower oil

Put the egg yolks, lemon juice or vinegar and salt into a food processor or bowl.

Process or whisk by hand. With the motor running, or while still whisking vigorously add a thin, steady stream of olive oil and gradually increase the flow as the mayonnaise thickens, stopping when it has become thick and glossy. Fold in the parsley. (If the mayonnaise fails to emulsify, beat another egg yolk separately and add the curdled mayonnaise to the yolk little by little.)

11

REEN SAUCE

Green sauces based primarily upon olive oil, garlic and parsley are typical of southern Europe and are usually served as relishes for boiled fish and meat dishes such as Milanese *bollito misto*. This recipe makes enough for 4 and is also very good with *carpaccio*.

small bunch of fresh parsley, washed
1 clove of garlic, peeled
2-3 shallots or 1 small onion, peeled
2 tsp capers, rinsed and drained
1 stale slice of bread, soaked in water and squeezed
2 tbs wine vinegar
salt and freshly milled black pepper
6 tbs extra virgin olive oil

Combine all the ingredients except for 4 tbs of the oil in a food processor; process very briefly (the sauce should not be completely smooth). Stir in the reserved oil. The sauce will keep well if covered; in fact, the flavour will improve after an hour or so.

GRILLED (BROILED) MUSHROOMS

Large open cap mushrooms are delicious liberally dressed with olive oil, seasoned, stuffed with an aromatic mixture of parsley, shallots and garlic, and grilled. Serve one very large, or 2 slightly smaller caps per person, and accompany with crusty bread to mop up the delectable juices. Serves 4.

4-8 open cap mushrooms, wiped clean
4 cloves of garlic, peeled and finely chopped
2 shallots, peeled and very finely chopped
4 generous handfuls of fresh parsley, washed and chopped
extra virgin olive oil
salt and freshly milled black pepper

Pre-heat the grill (broiler). Chop the mushroom stems finely and combine them with the garlic, shallots and parsley. Arrange the mushroom caps on a clean baking pan, the stem sides facing up. Drizzle olive oil liberally over the mushrooms and season them with salt and pepper. Grill for about 3 minutes, then turn the mushrooms over, pour a little more oil over them, and season. Grill the tops for 4 minutes. Invert the mushrooms again so that the partly-cooked stem sides face upwards. Spoon the parsley mixture into the cavities and drizzle more oil over them. Grill again for 2-3 more minutes, spoon some of the pan juices over the mushrooms and serve immediately.

ℱUNGHI TRIFOLATI

Italians love to cook wild or cultivated mushrooms very simply, sautéed with olive oil, garlic and plenty of fresh parsley. (The origins of the name of this dish are unclear, but *trifolare* may mean 'to cook in the manner of truffles'.) Serve as an appetizer, or light lunch for 2 people, accompanied by a green salad and crusty bread. Use a single variety or a mixture of wild mushrooms, or substitute the more unusual cultivated varieties such as oyster mushrooms, organic brown caps, and meaty shiitake.

3 tbs extra virgin olive oil
1 dried red chili pepper, crumbled
350 g/12 oz mushrooms, cleaned and sliced (not too thinly)
2 cloves of garlic, peeled and chopped
salt and freshly milled black pepper
the leaves from 4-6 large sprigs of parsley, washed and chopped

Heat the oil in a well-seasoned or non-stick frying pan. Add the chili and the mushrooms and sauté over a medium heat for 5-6 minutes, turning them in the oil frequently. Add the garlic, season and continue to sauté for 2 more minutes. Throw in the parsley, mix well and serve.

CÈPES À LA BORDELAISE

This method of cooking porcini mushrooms is traditional to the Bordeaux region of France. You can substitute cultivated mushrooms, although the taste will be less intense. Serves 4.

675 g/1½ lb firm porcini or cultivated mushrooms
140 ml/5 fl oz/⅔ cup olive oil
4 cloves of garlic, peeled and chopped
salt and freshly milled black pepper
2 handfuls of fresh parsley, washed and chopped
juice of ½ a lemon or 4 tbs dry white wine

Clean the fungi by brushing or scraping away any dirt. Leave them whole if they are very small, otherwise slice them thickly. Heat the oil in a heavy saucepan (or seasoned frying pan) and put in the mushrooms. Sear them for 1-2 minutes, then reduce the heat. After about 5 minutes, add the garlic. Stir well and season. Continue to sauté for 5 more minutes, then add the parsley and lemon juice (or wine). Increase the heat to reduce the liquid, which will only take a few minutes. Serve with crusty bread.

MIXED SALAD WITH PARSLEY AND WILD GREENS

The pungent, minty leaves of flat-leaved parsley are wonderful in salads. Experiment with different ingredients for contrasts of colour and flavour. Edible flowers of rocket, nasturtium, borage or chives make an elegant embellishment to this substantial, delicious salad which serves 4.

1 red or yellow sweet pepper
2 carrots, scrubbed
2 sticks (ribs) of celery, trimmed and sliced
2 juicy tomatoes, quartered
small handful of tender young dandelion leaves
bunch of watercress
some fresh rocket (arugula) leaves
leaves from a small bunch of flat-leaved parsley
2 hard-boiled eggs, peeled and quartered
6 anchovy fillets (optional)
4-6 tbs extra virgin olive oil
2 tbs lemon juice
salt

Wash all the vegetables and leaves, shake off the excess moisture and pat them dry. Remove the cap, pith and seeds of the pepper; dice the flesh. Grate the carrots coarsely. Put the vegetables and leaves into a china, glass or earthenware bowl and combine them. Decorate with the egg quarters and lay on the anchovy fillets (if required). Beat the olive oil with the lemon juice and salt until smooth and creamy. Pour over the salad and mix thoroughly so that everything is properly coated with the dressing. Serve immediately.

BEANS AND SWEET CORN SALAD

This perfectly delicious and very healthy Mediterranean salad is remarkably easy to assemble if you use canned beans and corn. In season, by all means substitute young, tender broad (fava) beans and fresh corn sliced off the cob (both will require about 8 minutes' boiling). Serve with crusty bread to mop up the delectable juices. This recipe makes enough for 4 people.

500 g/14 oz can of red kidney beans, rinsed and drained
500 g/14 oz can of cannellini, borlotti or flageolet beans, rinsed and drained
500 g/14 oz can of sweet corn, rinsed and drained
8 sun-dried tomatoes in oil, sliced into thin strips
6 shallots, peeled and thinly sliced
or 1 red or white onion, peeled, halved from top to bottom and thinly sliced
2 cloves of garlic, peeled and finely chopped
6 tbs extra virgin olive oil
juice of half a lemon
salt and freshly milled black pepper
2 hard-boiled eggs, shelled and quartered
leaves from a small bunch of flat-leaved parsley, washed

Combine the beans, corn, tomatoes, shallots (or onion) and garlic in a salad bowl. Beat the oil with the lemon juice, salt and pepper and pour over the salad, mixing thoroughly. Decorate with the eggs and parsley and serve with crusty bread.

HAMBURG PARSLEY AND CELERIAC (CELERY ROOT) SOUP

Hamburg parsley is grown primarily for its root which tastes a little like celeriac and resembles a thin parsnip. The roots are very good ingredients in delicate soups but can also be cooked like carrots and served as a vegetable accompaniment. If you cannot find Hamburg parsley, substitute Jerusalem (root) artichokes and just before serving, stir in a handful of parsley leaves for flavour.

225 g/8 oz Hamburg parsley roots, cleaned
or 225 g/8 oz Jerusalem artichokes, cleaned
350 g/12 oz piece of celeriac
25 g/1 oz butter
2 tbs extra virgin olive oil
1 medium onion, peeled and chopped
1 clove of garlic, peeled and chopped
salt and freshly milled black pepper
900 ml/2 pints home-made chicken or
vegetable stock
4 tbs double (heavy) cream

Carefully peel the Hamburg parsley (or Jerusalem artichokes) and celeriac and cut them into small chunks. Slice the chunks. Melt the butter in a pot with the olive oil. Soften the onion, add the garlic and root vegetables and sauté until lightly coloured (this will take just a few minutes). Season and add the stock. Bring to the boil, then reduce to a simmer, cover the pot and cook for an hour. Correct the seasoning if necessary and allow the soup to cool a little. Liquidize it thoroughly in a food processor, re-heat gently

18

and stir in the cream. (Add some fresh parsley leaves if Jerusalem artichokes have been substituted.) Serve very hot, with croûtons.

$\mathscr{M}$INESTRA PRIMAVERA

In Italy, tender, late spring vegetables are celebrated in a variety of delicious, healthy soups, sometimes with a liberal quantity of fresh parsley added to accentuate their freshness. This makes more than enough soup for 4 people.

225 g/8 oz green beans
675 g/1½ lb tender young broad (fava) beans
or 300 g/11 oz canned broad or flageolet beans
3 tbs extra virgin olive oil
2 cloves of garlic, peeled and chopped
whole white parts of 8 large spring onions (scallions)
or the white parts of a bunch of small ones
tender heart of a celery, sliced
salt and freshly milled black pepper
1 litre/2¼ pints water or vegetable stock
175 g/6 oz Swiss chard, washed and shredded
or fresh spinach leaves, washed and shredded
small bunch of flat-leaved parsley, washed and chopped

Wash the green beans and snap off their ends. Cut them into 2 cm/1 inch sections. Shell the broad beans (or rinse and drain the canned beans). Heat the oil in a pot. Sauté all the vegetables except for the Swiss chard (or spinach) for 3 minutes, turning them over from time to time. Season and pour in the water (or vegetable stock). Bring to the boil, then reduce the heat, cover and simmer for about 10 minutes. Throw in the Swiss chard (or spinach) and simmer for a few minutes longer. Stir in the parsley, and serve with a bowl of freshly-grated parmesan or *pecorino* cheese and hunks of crusty bread.

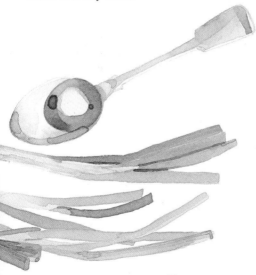

$\mathscr{L}$INGUINE ALLE VONGOLE

Molluscs and pasta are often served together in many parts of Italy. Although clams are the most common ingredient, other shellfish – whelks, winkles and mussels – are often used as well. Mussels, which are easier to find, are a good substitute because they are prepared and cooked in exactly the same way as clams. Serves 4.

675 g/1½ lb clams or mussels
400 g/14 oz linguine or spaghetti
4 tbs olive oil
4 cloves of garlic, peeled and chopped
1 small dried chili pepper, crumbled
450 g/1 lb very ripe fresh plum tomatoes, peeled and chopped
or 400 g/14 oz canned plum tomatoes, chopped
1 small glass of white wine
salt and freshly milled black pepper
small bunch of flat-leaved parsley, washed and chopped

22

Sort the clams, discarding any that are not tightly closed. Scrub and wash them in plenty of fresh water. Rinse them well and tip them into a pot of boiling water, cover and boil for 5 minutes. The shells should open; discard any that don't. Heat a very large pot of salted water to a vigorous boil. Immerse the pasta and boil until *al dente*. Meanwhile, heat the olive oil in a saucepan. Mix in the garlic and chili, quickly add the tomatoes and wine, and season. Reduce to a thick sauce. Put aside until the pasta is tender. Drain the pasta well. Add the clams and parsley to the sauce, re-heat it quickly and mix thoroughly with the pasta. Transfer to a warmed serving bowl and serve immediately, with crusty bread.

SPAGHETTI AL OLIO, AGLIO E PREZZEMOLO

This simple spaghetti dish from southern Italy requires no cheese but plenty of bread to mop up the delicious, garlicky oil. Flat-leaved or curly parsley may be used, although the former is more authentic. Serves 4.

400 g/14 oz spaghetti
5 tbs extra virgin olive oil
2 cloves of garlic, peeled and chopped
1 dried chili pepper, crumbled
salt
generous handful of parsley, washed and chopped

Bring plenty of salted water to a vigorous boil in a large pot. Add the spaghetti, stir well and cook until *al dente*. Meanwhile, heat the oil in a small frying pan and add the garlic, chilli and a pinch of salt. Fry very gently for less than a minute, then throw in the parsley before the garlic burns. As soon as the parsley crackles, remove the pan from the heat. When the pasta is ready, drain it well and put it into a warmed serving bowl. Quickly re-heat the oil and pour it over the pasta, mixing well. Serve at once.

$\mathscr{P}$ASTA WITH A CREAMY PARSLEY SAUCE

Serve this sauce with any factory-made durum wheat pasta shapes, cooked until *al dente* and well drained. The sauce is sufficient for 4 servings of pasta.

50 g/2 oz butter
2 cloves of garlic, peeled and finely chopped
2 fresh ripe plum tomatoes, peeled and diced
400 g/14 oz pasta
salt and freshly milled black pepper
225 ml/8 fl oz/1 cup double (heavy) cream
small bunch (about 6 sprigs) of fresh parsley, washed and chopped
110 g/4 oz piece of parmesan, freshly grated

Melt the butter in a pan with the garlic. Immediately add the tomatoes and cook gently for about 4 minutes while you bring a very large pot of salted water to a rolling boil. Add the pasta to the boiling water, mix and cook until just tender. Meanwhile, season the tomato and garlic mixture and add the cream. Cook for a minute or so to allow the cream to thicken slightly. Add the parsley and mix well. Drain and return the pasta to the empty pot (or transfer to a warmed serving bowl). Mix the sauce and half of the parmesan thoroughly with the pasta, and serve with the remaining cheese in a separate bowl.

$\mathcal{N}$ETTLE (OR SPINACH) AND PARSLEY PASTA

Tender young nettle shoots can be gathered with gardening gloves in the spring before they flower. Combined with parsley, they add wonderful colour and flavour to fresh egg pasta. However, if you distrust nettles, you can always substitute spinach. Serve the green noodles (enough for 4) with a tomato sauce and plenty of freshly grated parmesan cheese.

NETTLE PURÉE
175 g/6 oz nettle shoots or spinach leaves
small bunch of fresh parsley
2 tbs water

Wash the nettles (or spinach leaves) thoroughly. Put them into a small pot and cook them in the water that clings to them until they have wilted to a pulp. Put the pulp into a food processor with the parsley and water and process to a purée.

PASTA
350 g/12 oz extra fine plain (all-purpose) flour
3 eggs
1 tsp salt
1 tbs olive oil

Pour the flour into a bowl and make a well in the centre. Break the eggs into the well. Add the salt, olive oil and the nettle purée. Knead with floured hands for 15 minutes, with a machine fitted with dough hooks for 5 minutes, or in a food processor (the dough will roll up into a smooth ball

26

in less than a minute and will need brief additional hand-working). If necessary, apply a little more flour and continue to knead until the dough is elastic and smooth. Let it rest for about 10 minutes.

Apply a sprinkling of flour to a large, clean work surface, and to the surface of a rolling pin. Roll the dough out as thinly as possible, without breaking it. Let the sheet of pasta dry out for about half an hour, sprinkle with a little flour, then roll it up like a carpet, and cut it crossways with a sharp knife at equal intervals of ³⁄₄ cm/¹⁄₄ inch. Unravel the noodles, carefully drape them over the back of a chair and leave them to dry a little longer (if you want to store them, let them dry out completely overnight). Alternatively, the dough sheet can be left flat and cut with a knife (or with a pastry wheel which will leave attractive saw-toothed edges).

$\mathscr{V}$ICHY CARROTS

Carrots boiled in a little salted and sugared buttery water become glazed in the residue once the liquid has boiled away. Plenty of fresh chopped parsley and a generous sprinkling of freshly milled black pepper finish off this dish which goes very well with most meat and poultry. Ample for 4.

900 g/2 lb carrots, trimmed and scrubbed
water, to just cover the carrots
25 g/1 oz butter
$\frac{1}{2}$ tsp salt
$\frac{1}{2}$ tsp sugar
generous handful of fresh parsley, washed and chopped
freshly milled black pepper

Chop the carrots into even segments about 1 cm/$\frac{1}{2}$ inch thick. (Baby carrots can be left whole, preferably with the very bottom of their leaves still attached.) Transfer them to a pan. Barely cover them with water. Add the butter, salt and sugar, and bring to the boil. Cook, uncovered, until the water has boiled away. Stirring frequently, glaze the carrots in the sweet buttery residue, until lightly coloured. Add the parsley and black pepper, mix well and serve.

$\mathscr{P}$EPERONATA

These stewed sweet peppers are very popular all over Italy where they are usually served as an *antipasto*. Serve as a vegetable accompaniment to roasts or grills or eat them with bread. Serves 4.

4 large sweet peppers (red, yellow, orange, or mixed)
1 onion, peeled
6 tbs extra virgin olive oil
3 cloves of garlic, peeled and chopped
450 g/1 lb fresh ripe plum tomatoes, peeled and chopped
or 400 g/14 oz canned tomatoes, chopped
1 glass of white wine
salt and freshly milled black pepper
generous handful of flat-leaved parsley, washed and chopped

Remove and discard the caps, pithy membrane and seeds of the peppers. Slice the flesh into finger-wide strips. Halve the onion from top to bottom and slice each hemisphere thinly. Heat the olive oil in a pan with the onion and garlic. Sauté gently until the onion is soft and pale golden. Add the peppers, tomatoes and wine, season and cover the pan. Cook gently for about 25 minutes, stirring occasionally to prevent the bottom from burning. Mix in the parsley and serve. (If served cold, the *peperonata* benefits from a little additional olive oil dribbled over it.)

$\mathscr{P}$OTATO AND PARSLEY CAKES

These French *galettes* are similar to Swiss *rösti* and American hash browns. The potatoes are parboiled, grated and cooked with onion, egg and parsley until crisp and golden on the outside while retaining a soft interior. Potato varieties which are particularly suited to frying, such as Red désirée, work best, although 'general-purpose' potatoes can be used. Serve very hot, either on their own, or as a vegetable accompaniment, for 4 people.

575 g/1¼ lb medium-sized potatoes
2 eggs
3 tbs grated gruyère or cheddar cheese
salt and freshly milled black pepper
generous handful of fresh parsley, washed and chopped
4 tbs olive oil, for frying
1 medium onion, peeled and finely chopped
1 clove of garlic, peeled and chopped

Parboil the unpeeled potatoes for just 10 minutes. When cool, peel off their skins and grate them into thin discs through the widest blade of the grater (or slice them very finely with a sharp knife). Transfer the potatoes to a bowl. Beat the eggs and mix them with the potatoes, adding the cheese, seasoning, and parsley. Pre-heat the grill (broiler).

Heat the olive oil in a very large, well-seasoned or non-stick frying pan (or divide between two smaller frying pans). Add the onion and garlic, reduce the heat and sauté until lightly coloured. Tip in the potato mixture, raise the heat, and stir thoroughly. Flatten the mixture with a wood-

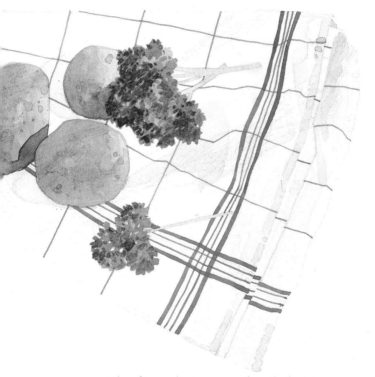

en spoon or spatula; after a minute or so, reduce the heat to
medium. Continue to cook for a few minutes longer, then
grill (broil) until the surface is golden. Serve hot.

$\mathcal{P}$ARSLEY OMELETTES

These omelettes are quick, delicious and colourful, contrasting a moist, rich green filling with a golden exterior. They make an ideal light lunch served with a crisp green salad and bread. Cook and serve each omelette separately. The quantities given are for one omelette; repeat according to the number of people to be served.

leaves of 3 large sprigs of parsley, washed and chopped
3 very fresh, free-range eggs
25 g/1 oz knob of butter
pinch of salt

Lightly beat half of the parsley into the eggs. Heat a small, well-seasoned or non-stick frying pan, add half the butter, and when it is about to change colour pour in the parslied egg mixture. Season with a little salt, add the remaining parsley and tip the pan, first to one side, and then to the other. When the eggs have almost completely set, fold it in three. Slide the omelette onto a barely warmed plate and top with the remaining knob of butter.

CHICKEN BREASTS IN LIME AND PARSLEY SAUCE

The chicken breasts are cooked in a delightfully sour, vivid green sauce that should be just dense enough to cling without swamping them. Serves 4 people accompanied by sautéed potatoes, and a vegetable. I like to serve this with crisp polenta; this is cooked polenta that is allowed to set, then cut into oblongs and shallow-fried.

4 tbs extra virgin olive oil
4 corn-fed or free-range chicken breasts, skins on
2 cloves of garlic, peeled and roughly chopped
4 tbs dry white wine
juice of 2 limes and the zest of 1 lime
salt and freshly milled black pepper
2 handfuls of fresh parsley, washed and finely chopped

Heat the olive oil to smoking point in a non-stick frying pan. Reduce the heat and slip in the chicken breasts. Fry them gently until golden all over (about 5 minutes), then add the garlic, wine, lime juice and zest, and seasoning. Mix well and raise the heat to medium, spooning the sauce over the chicken breasts. Reduce the heat to minimum once the liquid starts to thicken and continue to simmer, uncovered, for 10-12 minutes, spooning more sauce over the chicken from time to time. You will be left with a very concentrated sauce. Sprinkle with the parsley and serve.

$\mathcal{R}$OAST CHICKEN WITH PARSLEY STUFFING

This is a tastier Gallic version of our traditional Sunday roast chicken with bread sauce. The stuffing is wonderfully moist and aromatic. Serves 4.

2 tbs olive oil
1 onion, peeled and finely chopped
6 cloves of garlic, peeled and roughly chopped
4 tbs crushed tomatoes
salt and freshly milled black pepper
splash of white wine
60 g/3 oz fresh breadcrumbs
small bunch of flat-leaved parsley, washed and chopped
1 large roasting chicken
freshly milled black pepper
4 tbs olive oil
4 tbs white wine
salt
1 small glass of white wine

Pre-heat the oven to 200° C/400° F/Gas Mark 6.

Heat the olive oil and sauté the onion and garlic until soft and pale golden. Mix in the tomatoes and season. Cook for 2 more minutes. Remove from the heat, moisten with wine and mix in the breadcrumbs and all but 1 tbs of the parsley. Place the chicken on a roasting tin (pan) and season inside and out with black pepper. Stuff the cavity with the parsley mixture. Pour the olive oil and 4 tbs of wine over the bird and roast for 30 minutes, basting occasionally. Turn carefully and continue to roast for 45 minutes. (Towards the end of the roasting time, sprinkle the chicken with salt.) Drain the roasting juices into a small pan, add the remaining wine and reduce while the chicken 'rests' for a few minutes. Add the reserved parsley to the sauce. Carve and serve the chicken with the stuffing and the sauce.

$\mathscr{P}$OACHED FILLETS OF SOLE WITH AN EDWARDIAN PARSLEY SAUCE

The traditional English accompaniment to poached fish is parsley sauce, for which I have adapted a recipe from my 1909 edition of *Mrs Beeton's Book of Household Management*. Dover sole is especially delicious but lemon sole or any succulent, flat white fish fillets may be substituted. Ask the fishmonger to fillet the fish and save the bones and trimmings for the stock (broth). The following recipes will make enough for 4.

FISH STOCK
1 litre/2¼ pints water
bones and trimmings from 900 g/2 lb fresh Dover sole
2 carrots, scrubbed and chopped
1 stick (rib) of celery, washed and chopped
1 onion, chopped
1 tsp tomato purée (paste)
2 sprigs of thyme and parsley
1 bay leaf
salt and freshly milled black pepper

Bring the water to a boil in a pot. Add the remaining ingredients and bring to a simmer. Cover the pot and cook the stock for about an hour, removing from time to time the scum that rises to the surface. Strain the stock, reserve the quantity required and freeze the surplus in plastic food bags.

PARSLEY SAUCE
25 g/1 oz butter
2 tbs plain (all-purpose) flour
280 ml/10 fl oz/1¼ cups fish stock (see above)
2 tbs dry white wine
salt and freshly milled black pepper
small bunch of parsley, washed and finely chopped

Stir the butter and the flour over a medium heat for a few minutes. Stir in the fish stock and wine, bring to the boil, reduce the heat, cover and simmer for about 10 minutes. Season and stir in the parsley. To preserve the bright green colour of the herb, the sauce should be served at once with the poached fish fillets.

POACHED SOLE FILLETS
900 g/2 lb sole, filleted
1 carrot, scrubbed and roughly chopped
1 onion, peeled and quartered
1 stick of celery
1 bay leaf
sprig of fresh parsley
10 black peppercorns

Wash the fillets and pat them dry. Roll them up tightly and secure with wooden toothpicks. Heat the other ingredients in enough water to cover the rolled fillets. Bring them to a simmer and after 15 minutes, add the fish. Poach for about 10 minutes and serve on warmed plates accompanied by the parsley sauce, boiled new potatoes and a vegetable. Garnish with lemon wedges.

$\mathscr{P}$ARSLIED FISH CAKES

Once considered to be nursery food, fish cakes now grace the menus of the most chic restaurants, and are delicious when they have been prepared properly. This old-fashioned recipe makes enough for 4 and can be made with any firm, white-fleshed fish fillets, or with fresh salmon steaks. Serve with Scandinavian mustard sauce.

SCANDINAVIAN MUSTARD SAUCE
1 tbs prepared English mustard
1 tbs sugar
1 tbs white wine vinegar
salt and freshly milled pepper
1 egg yolk, at room temperature
6 tbs light vegetable oil
4 tbs sour cream
handful of fresh dill, chopped

Combine the mustard, sugar and vinegar, season to taste with salt and pepper, and beat in the egg yolk. Whisk or process, adding the oil in a thin, steady stream.

When it is thick, finish the sauce by folding in the sour cream and fresh dill. Spoon into a serving bowl and reserve.

COURT BOUILLON
1 carrot, scrubbed and roughly chopped
1 onion, peeled and quartered
1 stick of celery
1 bay leaf
sprig of fresh parsley
10 black peppercorns

FISH CAKES
575 g/1¼ lb white fish fillets
350 g/12 oz floury potatoes, peeled, boiled until soft, and mashed
1 tsp capers, rinsed, drained and finely chopped
1 tbs mustard powder
2 tbs soy sauce
salt and freshly milled white pepper
2 handfuls of fresh parsley, washed and finely chopped
60 g/3 oz plain (all-purpose) flour
oil for frying

Heat the *court bouillon* ingredients in enough water to cover the fish. Bring them to a simmer and after 15 minutes, add the fish. Poach until the flesh flakes (8-10 minutes). Remove and mash the flesh with a fork. Combine the mashed fish and potatoes, add the remaining fish cake ingredients, except for half of the flour and the oil, and mix very thoroughly. With floured hands, shape the mixture into eight cakes, rolling them in the remaining flour, to coat. Heat the oil in a non-stick frying pan. Slip in the fish cakes and fry them until golden brown on both sides. Serve with the Scandinavian mustard sauce.

ESTOFADO DE TERNERA

This delicious Spanish stew is thickened towards the end of the cooking time with an aromatic Catalan *picada*, made here with pine nuts, parsley, saffron and garlic. Jointed game birds, rabbit or poultry can be substituted for veal, but reduce the cooking time accordingly and allow any excess liquid to boil off. Serve with puréed potatoes. Makes enough for 4 people.

PICADA
2 cloves of garlic, peeled
50 g / 2 oz pine nuts
pinch of saffron strands
6 sprigs of flat-leaved parsley, washed
2 tbs extra virgin olive oil
pinch of salt

Pound the ingredients to a paste with a mortar and pestle, or grind everything together in a food processor. Put the *picada* to one side.

ESTOFADO
4 tbs olive oil
675 g / 1¼ lb lean veal, evenly cubed
1 large onion, peeled and chopped
1 carrot, scrubbed and diced
1 stick (rib) of celery, trimmed and diced
1 heaped tbs tomato purée (paste)
225 ml / 8 fl oz / 1 cup water
4 tbs dry sherry
salt and freshly milled black pepper
175 g / 6 oz button mushrooms, quartered

Heat the olive oil in a large casserole with a lid. Brown the veal evenly and transfer to a plate. Soften the onion, carrot and celery in the oil. Return the veal to the casserole, add the tomato purée, pour in the water and the sherry, season, and bring to the boil. Reduce the heat, cover, and simmer for 1¼ hours. Add the mushrooms and the *picada*, mix well and continue to simmer for 15 minutes longer. Serve immediately.

PARSLEY